Sound It Out

Complex Vowels

by Wiley Blevins
illustrated by Sean O'Neill

Red Chair Press   Egremont, Massachusetts

Look! Books are produced and published by Red Chair Press:

Red Chair Press LLC   PO Box 333   South Egremont, MA 01258-0333

www.redchairpress.com

 FREE activity page from www.redchairpress.com/free-activities

Wiley Blevins is an early-reading specialist and author of the best-selling *Phonics from A to Z: A Practical Guide* from Scholastic and *A Fresh Look at Phonics* from Corwin. Wiley has taught elementary school in both the United States and in South America. He has written more than 70 books for children and 15 for teachers, as well as created reading programs for schools in the U.S. and Asia.

Publisher's Cataloging-In-Publication Data

Names: Blevins, Wiley. | O'Neill, Sean, 1968- illustrator.

Title: Complex vowels / by Wiley Blevins ; illustrated by Sean O'Neill.

Description: Egremont, Massachusetts : Red Chair Press, [2019] | Series: Look! books : Sound it out | Includes word-building examples. | Interest age level: 004-008. | Summary: "Vowel teams can make both long and complex vowel sounds. The special complex vowel teams can be spelled in many different ways. They can be used to build common words we use every day. Readers discover what these complex vowels can do."--Provided by publisher.

Identifiers: ISBN 9781634403412 (library hardcover) | ISBN 9781634403535 (paperback) | ISBN 9781634403474 (ebook)

Subjects: LCSH: English language--Vowels--Juvenile literature. | English language--Pronunciation--Juvenile literature. | CYAC: English language--Vowels. | English language--Pronunciation.

Classification: LCC PE1157 .B54 2019 (print) | LCC PE1157 (ebook) | DDC 428.13--dc23

LCCN: 2017963414

Illustrations by Sean O'Neill

Photo credits: iStock except for pg. 11: Ingimage

Printed in the United States of America

0918 1P CGBS19

Vowels can make short sounds. These vowels are often alone in words like <u>a</u> in c<u>a</u>t.

Vowels can make long sounds, too. Some long vowel sounds work in teams like <u>ai</u> in tr<u>ai</u>n.

Table of Contents

Lots of vowel teams make long sounds.

But some make special sounds.

They are neither short nor long.

So listen up!

We don't want to get these sounds wrong.

Twinkle, twinkle little <u>star</u>,
How I wonder what you <u>are</u>.

Both st<u>ar</u> and <u>are</u>
have the "ar" sounds.

This is a special team.

It is made up of a vowel
plus the letter <u>r</u>.

You say this team
like a grumpy pirate.

Aaarrrgh!

Are you ready for more?

Both for and more
have the "or" sounds.

So do shore, fork,
and storm.

These are more teams
made up of a vowel
plus the letter r.

But they are not
the last ones.

Say these words:
h<u>er</u>, f<u>ir</u>st, t<u>ur</u>tle.

Listen closely.

Three vowel teams make the
"ur" sounds: <u>er</u>, <u>ir</u>, and <u>ur</u>.

How do you know which
to use to write a word?

You must remember the
words. Lots of reading
and writing help.

Now say these words:
b<u>oy</u>, b<u>oi</u>l.

The vowel teams <u>oy</u> and <u>oi</u> make the same sound. *Oy!*

That's a fun sound to say.

But look carefully.

The <u>oi</u> spelling never comes at the end of a word.

That will help you spell words with this sound.

OWWW! is the sound you make when something really hurts.

You can spell the "ou" sound with two vowel teams: <u>ou</u> and <u>ow</u>.

Listen: r<u>ou</u>nd, h<u>ou</u>se, t<u>ow</u>n, n<u>ow</u>.

Do you want to know a secret?

The <u>ou</u> spelling never comes at the end of a word.

That will help you spell words with this sound, too.

G<u>oo</u>d. G<u>oo</u>se. B<u>oo</u>k. B<u>oo</u>t.

Wait a minute!

All these words have
the team <u>oo</u> in them.

But something is different.

The vowel team <u>oo</u> can
make two different sounds.

Oo! I bet you already
knew that.

Goose Goose G<u>EE</u>SE?

We're almost done.

You just <u>saw</u>
many special vowel teams.

But <u>saw</u> and <u>sauce</u> have
other important ones to learn.

Both <u>aw</u> and <u>au</u>
make the "aw" sound.

You can find it in my
favorite word: *dinos<u>au</u>r*.

RAWR!

Let's Build Words

Let's have some fun with these special vowel teams. Let's build some words.

Say the sound for <u>m</u>.
Now say the sound for <u>oo</u>.
Put the two sounds together.
What word did you make?

Moo!

Wow! You sound like a cow.

Do you live on a f<u>ar</u>m
in a b<u>ar</u>n?

Let's try another one.
Start with <u>barn</u>.
Change the <u>n</u> to <u>k</u>.
What word did you make?

Moo!

23

BARK!

Now you sound like a dog.
A h<u>ou</u>nd. A p<u>oo</u>ch.

Okay. No more animal noises.
Say the word <u>mouth</u>.
What do you say it
with? Your mouth,
of course!

Let's play with
the word <u>mouth</u>.

Change the letters
<u>th</u> to <u>se</u>.

What new word
did you make?

You made a mouse.
Squeak!

Oops. That's another animal sound.

Let's fix it fast.

Look at <u>mouse</u>.

Change the <u>m</u> to <u>h</u>.

What word did you make now?

Yes. It's where that mouse
lives: its HOUSE!

Oh, no. Who is peeking
around the corner?

A cat!
Look at the mouse run.
It is running to
its little mouse house.

So, it's time for us
to say goodbye!

A mouse
in a house.

You've learned a lot about vowel teams. Vowel teams can make long sounds. They can make special sounds, too.

Take a close look at the vowel team in a word. Think about words you know with the same team. Then think about the sound the team makes. Use that sound to read the word. You're sure to get it right!

COOK BOOK